NOTRE DAME

Published by Abdo & Daughters, 6537 Cecilia Circle, Bloomington, Minnesota 55435.

Library bound edition distributed by Rockbottom Books, Pentagon Tower, P.O. Box 36036, Minneapolis, Minnesota 55435.

Library of Congress Number: 88-71724   ISBN: 0-939179-51-2

Cover photo by Notre Dame Photographic Department.
Inside photos by Notre Dame Photographic Department, except for page 37, Johnathan Daniels.

The author acknowledges the cooperation of Richard W. Conklin, Assistant Vice President, University Relations, University of Notre Dame, in providing information and photographs for this book.

Photo on page one is Washington Hall, Notre Dame's performing arts building.

UNIVERSITY
OF
NOTRE DAME

by Paul J. Deegan

The best known of America's church-affiliated universities, it was founded by a religious community formed in France. It achieved fame in the 1920s through its football team, and has concentrated during the past few decades on building its academic prowess.

This movement toward academic excellence was directed by a priest who served as the university's president for 35 years while becoming perhaps the most respected and best known of the nation's college leaders. When he retired in the spring of 1987, he was succeeded by a fellow priest who once played on the university's basketball team.

This university has some 80,000 actual alumni and alumnae, and thousands more so-called subway alumni — men and women who identify with the school because of religion and football. This relates to the university being the most national of the country's universities — it has the highest percentage of students who live more than 1,000 miles away from a university, although a preponderance of the student body is from Midwestern and Middle Atlantic states.

The campus, a virtually self-contained city just north of the northwestern Indiana city of South Bend, is the second largest tourist attraction in Indiana after the Indianapolis Motor Speedway.

Today the University of Notre Dame is home to some 7,600 young men and women who are undergraduates. There are also over 2,100 graduate and professional students at Notre Dame. The teaching and research faculty numbers some 1,000 people. The four colleges include 44 major areas of study.

NOTRE DAME HISTORY

Today's Notre Dame traces back to a late November day in 1842 when Father Edward Sorin, a young French priest, and three or four companions first looked over snow-covered land on which there were three buildings — a log chapel and cabin, a clapboard house, and a small log shed. It was the site of today's campus.

The then 28-year-old priest and his companions in a religious community had just completed a difficult 250-mile overland journey in 10 days. Because of the snow cover, the men didn't realize that the large tract of property, which had been acquired by the Catholic church and was being used as a mission, included two lakes. Not far away

was the village of South Bend, then home to about 1,000 people.

Sorin and his companions were members of a religious community recently founded at Le Mans in western France and which by 1857 would be called the Congregation of Holy Cross. Father Sorin was a Breton, born in a village near Laval, the son of a middle-class farming family. He had been sent to Indiana a year earlier, 25 years after Indiana had become the 19th state. He had been sent by his religious superior, Basil Anthony Moreau, who founded the community. Father Moreau was acceding to the request of another French priest who in 1834 had been named bishop of a newly created diocese (Vincennes) in Indiana.

The steeples of Sacred Heart Church on a wintry Indiana day.

Father Sorin had come to Indiana with six brothers (professed members of a religious community who are not clerics). None of the seven spoke English. A year later, Father Sorin had made the journey from southern Indiana to sparsely settled northern Indiana at the outermost limits of the diocese because he wanted to build a college. The bishop had promised the priest that his religious community would be given title to the property — over 500 acres — if within two years he could revive what had been a mission station, establish a program of formation for brothers, and build his college.

Soon after his arrival, Sorin renamed the site in the language of his native France, calling it Notre Dame du Lac (Our Lady of the Lake). That name also was to become the name of the university he developed.

The priest and the brothers soon began to build another log house, felling trees on the

Log chapel on Notre Dame campus recalls school's founding by a French missionary.

site for the lumber. However, the cold northern Indiana winter put a stop to the building until the spring of 1843. In February of that year 11 more brothers arrived from Vincennes. Sorin dedicated the log house a month later. It was to be the first of 34 buildings Sorin would construct in creating the Notre Dame campus.

Before the end of 1844, the community had established a Catholic men's college, a preparatory high school, a type of vocational school, and the house of formation for the brothers. The students were few in number. Notre Dame in 1844 had 25 students for whom tuition was $100 and room and board $65. There were eight faculty members.

But Sorin had met his goal and his religious community got title to the land as he had been promised. And the building continued with several buildings constructed around St. Mary's Lake, the smaller of the two lakes on the Notre Dame property. The first of these buildings was a two-story brick structure. Later expanded to four stories, it is known today as "Old College" and is the only surviving structure on the campus from the university's first decade.

During the Civil War, the governor of Indiana asked Sorin to provide chaplains for the Union Army. Among the eight Holy Cross priests who became chaplains was a future president of the university, William J. Corby, whose name later designated a residence hall. Corby served two terms as president He followed Sorin in 1866 and concluded his second term in 1881.

When Sorin's presidency ended in 1865, there was a college, and preparatory, grade, and trade schools, as well as religious institutions at Notre Dame. When he founded Notre Dame, there were only nine other Catholic colleges in the United States. By 1961 there were 51. Only seven of those colleges remain in existence today. Notre Dame beat the odds for many reasons, not the least of which was its proximity (90 miles) to the rapidly growing city of Chicago.

Sorin continued his tight control over Notre Dame after leaving the presidency. He became chairman of the university's Board of Trustees. In 1869 he decided to replace the major campus church, Sacred Heart, with a bigger one. The drawings of the church, which took more than 15 years to complete, resembled the church in Sorin's hometown in France.

Father Sorin has been called a "dreamer-builder." He remained the principal policy-maker for the university until he died in 1893. However, in 1879 when Father Sorin was 65 and serving as the worldwide head of the Holy Cross community as well as still chairing Notre Dame's Board of Trustees, the dream momentarily gave way to a nightmare. A fire swept through the six-story Main Building, which was really the entire college facility.

When Sorin was notified in Montreal, he abandoned a planned trip abroad and returned to look over the ruins of his life's work. As one who was present recalled, he indicated he wanted those present to go into

Edward Sorin, C.S.C., founding father of Notre Dame.

the campus church with him. He stood at the altar steps, and said, "If it were all gone, I should not give up."

Sorin had decided that when he founded the university as a young man, he had "dreamed too small a dream. Tomorrow," he said, "we will begin again and build it bigger, and when it is built, we will put a gold dome on top with a golden statue of the Mother of God . . ."

"There was never more a shadow of doubt as to the future of Notre Dame," wrote the man who had been present when Sorin spoke. Later it was written that ". . . historians have argued that while Sorin founded the university on a cold winter afternoon in 1842, he also refounded it on a fresh April Sunday in 1879. His resolve to build again inspired similar communal determination."

The fire was on April 23. Fewer than four months later, a new administration building — with classrooms, offices, and dormitories — was ready for the fall semester. Three hundred workers had kept at the job from dawn until sunset to finish the building by fall. The new building is said to "embody much of the cultural sytle and intellectual ambience of 19th-century Notre Dame." The building's golden dome and the statue were completed later.

That golden dome on top of the now century-old administration building has come to identify the university to its community and to others who have never even been there. The golden dome looks over a campus Father Sorin "envisioned, designed, and built" in the words of a Notre Dame historian. Six years after the turn of the century, a statue of Sorin was erected at the heart of the campus. "Like his statue, Sorin has become larger than life in Notre Dame history," the historian noted, "but the excess is not without its truth." He described Notre Dame's founder as "a man of salt and savvy, of great heart and great hope."

Sorin has been characterized as "shrewd, opinionated, and adventuresome." He recognized the importance of mail to a rural, residential college, and he also knew that if Notre Dame was a postal station, the campus would appear on all official government maps. In 1851 he acquired a postal station for Notre Dame.

Well before the days of air travel, Sorin made the trip between Indiana and Europe 52 times. Also an astute businessman, Sorin, by his death at 78 in 1893, had, according to a history of Notre Dame, "parlayed the 524 acres, $300, and a line of limited credit" he had been given by the bishop in 1842 "into an extensive portfolio of landholdings and investments so complex that it took 18 years finally to settle his estate."

At the time of it's founder's death, the academic tone at Notre Dame was "still that of a French boarding school," according to a history of the school. Students had communal study halls from 7 to 10 p.m., after which it was time for bed.

Salaries for lay faculty before the turn of the century "satisfied only the most dedicated," says one history of the school.

Notre Dame's Administration Building, topped by the famous Golden Dome.

However, the arts held a position of respect in 19th century Notre Dame. A play by Sophocles, performed in Greek, was the first performance at the new Washington Hall in 1882. The university's band is one of the oldest in continual existence. It was founded in 1846.

The first of the residence halls, Sorin Hall, was built in 1888. The university built it because Sorin and others had noticed that a few senior students who had private rooms — the rest of the students slept and studied in communal areas — excelled academically. So why not a hall with all private rooms? It would be followed over the years by the construction of some 30 more such halls, some later converted to other use.

It was in a first-floor room in Sorin Hall that two students, Michael and John Shea, in 1906 wrote one of the best-known of all school songs, *The Notre Dame Victory March*. The song's chorus, beginning "Cheer, cheer for old Notre Dame," is familiar to millions of Americans.

By the turn of the century, Notre Dame had become a self-sufficient "city", from farms to a firehouse and an infirmary. In 1902 railroad tracks of a private spur line ran to a spot behind the administration building. Passenger trains chartered by alumni clubs in the Midwest came on campus on football Saturdays. Along the tracks were coal yards, warehouses, ice houses, and even, at one time, a stockyard.

However, at this time Notre Dame was a university in name only. It was a preparatory school and college with fewer than a thousand students. A vocational trade school, originally established by Sorin for orphaned boys entrusted to his care and later called St. Joseph's Industrial School, was still in operation. However, early in the 1900s the curriculum began to expand with departments of journalism and "political economy" being added at the college level. Enrollment doubled.

An instigator in expanding Notre Dame's academic thrust in the early 1900s was John Zahm, a Holy Cross priest and Notre Dame professor who served terms as Holy Cross provincial and university vice-president. A physical chemist who also compiled a large Dante collection, he thought, according to one school historian, "Notre Dame should strive to become the university that its charter claimed it was."

Zahm saw the university as possibly "the intellectual center of the American West." He wanted the large undergraduate, graduate, and professional schools, libraries, and research facilities that Notre Dame has today. Others in the Holy Cross community didn't believe the school could compete with existing, well-endowed private universities.

It was no accident that during Zahm's time at Notre Dame, the first discipline to have its own building was the sciences. He helped design Science Hall, which opened in 1884

Fitzpatrick Hall of Engineering.

13

and where future students such as Julius A. Nieuwland, who later as a Notre Dame faculty member was to discover formulae that led to synthetic rubber, studied. The Science Hall building was converted in 1953 to a student center.

Engineering education had begun at Notre Dame in the late 1800s. Civil engineering had been added to the curriculum in 1873. Mechanical and electrical engineering departments followed. A building to house the "Institute of Technology" had opened in 1890.

Early in the present century — 1906 was the first full year in which he was in command — John W. Cavanaugh became Notre Dame's president. He led the university until 1919 and is credited with taking the initial steps to make Notre Dame "a university in fact as well as in name."

By 1920 the trade school was gone and there were 28 buildings on the Notre Dame campus, most of them on either side of a large quadrangle with the golden domed topped Administration Building on one end — the university's Main Quadrangle. Tuition was $170 and room and board just over $400.

It was also the time when Notre Dame gained national prominence for its football team. Knute Rockne's squad, led by the play of All-America George Gipp, won the unofficial Western Football championship for the second time. Years later in 1940 in the movie *Knute Rockne — All American,* Gipp was portrayed by future United States President Ronald Reagan. The movie launched Reagan's acting career.

Notre Dame's athletic teams, nicknamed the Fighting Irish — which always has been a misnomer — have captured the country's attention for decades. The football success Notre Dame enjoyed under Rockne brought national recognition and substantial income — football profits jumped from $235 in 1919 to $529,420 in 1929.

Receipts from the 1925 Rose Bowl game helped put up an addition that year to the 26-year-old Fieldhouse. The addition was a basketball annex with 6,000 seats and Notre Dame could then play its home games on campus instead of at the South Bend YMCA.

However, in recent decades the university's decision makers have worked to ensure that the focus on Notre Dame is not narrowed to the school's football team. The university says today that it's "ultimate goal" is "to become not simply a leading institution of higher education, but a leading institution that has held fast to the strength and wisdom of its Catholic essence."

The era of Rockne and Gipp was also the time of the brief administration of James Burns, Notre Dame's ninth president. This Holy Cross priest reorganized the university's management structure, finances, and curricula, and raised its educational standards. In the words of Notre Dame archivist and historian Thomas McAvoy, Burns was responsible for "a major revolution in the academic development of the institution."

Burns was the school's first president to hold an earned doctorate. A chemist, he valued scholarly research and academic excellence.

Knute Rockne.

Rockne Memorial Building provides athletic facilities for Notre Dame students and faculty.

Burns appointed individual deans of the newly established colleges of Arts and Letters, Science, Engineering, Law, and Commerce. He also established a Board of Associate Lay Trustees whose major task was to raise a $1 million endowment. This was the first time the university sought funds on a nationwide basis.

During the 1920s the university saw one of its major objectives begin to erode. Notre Dame wanted to be a residential campus. The residence halls were an essential part of life at Notre Dame. Each had priests in residence and each had its own chapel. The halls were also the basis of the school's large-scale intramural athletic program. But the number of post-World War I students exceeded the space available in the existing residence halls. So three new residence halls were constructed. Toward the end of the decade, in 1927, a huge Gothic building containing two large dining halls, each seating over a thousand students, was completed.

Until the time of World War II, mealtime at Notre Dame was a very structured affair. Dressed in suit coat or suit jacket and tie, the young men marched into the dining halls in formation and went to tables set with silver and china. They stood in silence until a grace before meals was said by a presiding university official. Then a bell rang, they all sat, and student waiters served soup. Then dinner was served. After a closing grace, the students quietly left the halls in orderly lines.

And those students who had to live off campus in the 1920s — about a third of the student body — were forbidden to have cars and could not visit certain areas, usually night spots, in South Bend. This ban was enforced by the school's patrolling prefect of discipline.

What today would be considered a very strict atmosphere still prevailed on campus in the 1930s, by which time most students were again on campus where four more residence halls had been built. Students in the halls arose at 6:30 a.m., there were required religious activities, study in the evening was compulsory, and lights were off at 11 p.m., an hour earlier for freshmen.

It was an environment where one-fourth of the lay faculty lived permanently in the residence halls, and where the university president still knew every graduating senior by name.

Between 1920 and the mid-1930s, Notre Dame's student body had tripled, a larger faculty was more qualified and included more laymen, the university's income was 50 times greater, and the administration was less stringently controlled by the Holy Cross community. Notre Dame, one observer has said, "was finally a totally collegiate institution with the foundation laid for the expansion of graduate instruction and research . . ."

In 1926, Nieuwland discussed publicly his catalytic polymerization of acetylene which led to the basic patents in the manufacture of neoprene, sythentic rubber. A major company took note of the professor's reseach and subsidized his work and paid him substantial consulting fees which Nieuwland, also a Holy Cross priest, used to upgrade the chemistry library. Royalty income from his patents was later used by the university to help construct Nieuwland Science Hall.

It was also during these years that Professor James A. Reyniers began his pioneering efforts with germfree animals. This work subsequently led to the establishment of the Laboratories of Bacteriology at the University of Notre Dame (LOBUND).

What was to immediately become a campus landmark was also built at this time. Notre Dame Stadium was completed in 1930. The original sod in the 59,000-seat stadium was moved there from Cartier Field because Notre Dame had not lost a game played at Cartier during the preceding 23 years. Cartier was the all-purpose athletic field on campus where Notre Dame had played its football games for 75 years (they lost 8-0 to the University of Michigan in their first intercollegiate game in 1887).

Notre Dame Stadium with library mural in background.

In 1932, Notre Dame's Graduate School was established officially though the university had for many years awarded a master of arts degree. By this time, too, laymen outnumbered religious on the faculty by three to one. The ratio had been equal only a decade before.

The fund raising begun in the 1920's, plus gifts from the Rockefeller and Carnegie foundations as well as revenue from the football program, enabled the university to spend over $5 million on campus buildings. These included the seven new residence halls, the building with the dining halls, the basketball gymnasium, the stadium, and four classroom buildings.

When Notre Dame celebrated its centennial in 1942, it was wartime. World War II put a damper on celebrating and war rationing halted most campus construction. There were 45 buildings on campus. By 1942 Notre Dame had over 3,000 students and nearly 340 faculty members. Enrollment was down from the peak figure of over 3,200 in 1930 due to the national economic depression of the 1930s and the drafting of young men to fight in the war. Tuition then was $330; room and board, $459.

War Memorial on Notre Dame campus with Golden Dome in background.

Activity on campus related to the war distinctly changed the school. An estimated 12,000 men completed officers training in various programs hosted on campus between 1942 and 1946. Their presence changed class schedules, brought cafeteria-style serving to the dining halls, and, for the first time, brought a significant amount of women onto the former all-male campus.

When the war ended, over one and one-half million veterans could resume or begin a college education funded by the federal government. Many were married. Notre Dame dropped its traditional policy against admitting married men as undergraduates and with the cooperation of the federal government erected temporary housing on campus for the married veterans, an area that became known as Vetville. The buildings were bulldozed in 1961 to prepare the building site for Memorial Library. New housing for married students was constructed by the university off the campus.

Leading Notre Dame in the immediate post-war years — 1946 to 1952 — was another John Cavanaugh — John J. Like his 13 predecessors and, to date, two successors, he was a priest in the Holy Cross community. Though a Notre Dame graduate, he entered the community after working in advertising. After studies in Rome, he returned to Notre Dame and served as a university vice president.

As president, Cavanaugh set out goals similar to President Burns some 25 years earlier. He set up the Notre Dame Foundation in 1947 with a goal to raise $25 million in 10 years. Money was to be used for buildings and to expand the endowment fund begun by Burns.

Like Burns, Cavanaugh also reorganized the university's administration. He named 32-year-old Theodore M. Hesburgh, a theology instructor and well-liked chaplain to the Vetville community, as executive vice president. Cavanaugh, too, wanted better academics at Notre Dame. A Notre Dame historian says that the "expansion of advanced studies and research became a high priority under Cavanaugh (he authorized the establishment of LOBUND), and the number of students in the Graduate School rose from 96 in 1946 to 450 in 1951."

Cavanaugh upset some of the faculty, whom the historian describes as "eager and dedicated, but still woefully underpaid," by indicating that he intended to recruit new faculty who would be superior to those then teaching at the university.

During the 1940s, Notre Dame was again the ranking collegiate football power. Under coach Frank Leahy, the Fighting Irish won four national championships and six times had no losses in a season. Leahy's teams once went almost five seasons without losing while building a 39-game win streak.

John J. Cavanaugh, C.S.C., former president of Notre Dame.

Theodore M. Hesburgh, C.S.C., Notre Dame President from 1952 to 1987, in front of the library named for him.

Meanwhile, one of the critical decisions facing Cavanaugh was whether Notre Dame should let its undergraduate enrollment expand from the pre-war total of 3,200. He and his advisors opted for growth. During his six year (1946-1952) term, enrollment increased over 60 percent to 5,200 students.

Cavanaugh also expanded Notre Dame's outreach to the general American education and foundation scenes, a practice expanded by his chosen successor, Hesburgh.

The Hesburgh era began in 1952. During his 35 years as president, Hesburgh seemed to become synomous with Notre Dame. A native of Syracuse, New York, Hesburgh entered Notre Dame and the Holy Cross community after graduating from high school in 1934. His abilities were recognized by his religious superiors while he was still an undergraduate student. After ordination, he completed his studies for a doctorate in theology and returned to Notre Dame in 1945 to teach. Seven years later, at age 35, he was president of the university.

A chronicler of Notre Dame says Hesburgh set himself three goals — build a first-rate undergraduate college and upgrade the graduate school, reorganize Notre Dame as a modern university, and create what in his estimation had heretofore been only an ideal, a Catholic university.

Hesburgh has been characterized as "brilliant, forceful, and charismatic." He also reached out as no Notre Dame representative previously had done. He traveled over 130,000 miles a year while involved in university, academic, civic, and church activities. He became an advisor to presidents and popes. He was a charter member of and later chairman of the United States Commission on Civil Rights. He served on the Carnegie Commission on the Future of Higher Education as well as the boards of directors of the Chase Manhattan Bank and the Rockefeller Foundation. He was to receive honorary degrees from over 50 colleges and universities and was honored by numerous awards.

A *Time* magazine cover subject, Hesburgh was Notre Dame's emissary to the nation and the world, and a most popular one at that.

At Notre Dame he implemented his goals by deciding to limit undergraduate enrollment, tighten entrance requirements, and reform curricula in some of the colleges. He recruited faculty with academic excellence in mind, and increased the role of the faculty in governing the university.

In 1958, 18 Notre Dame students won Woodrow Wilson Teaching Fellowships, the most at all but four other schools. In 1960, the Ford Foundation cited Notre Dame along with Stanford University and four other institutions as "rapidly improving universities." Each of the six would receive a $6 million grant if the school could raise another $12 million over three years.

This was the beginning of major fund raising under Hesburgh. Subsequent efforts in the 1960s raised an additional $80 million. The money raised during this period was used for faculty development, endowment of distinguished professorships, increased student aid, expansion of graduate education, the establishment of various area study projects and special projects such as the Institute for Advanced Religious Studies, and for new construction.

Notre Dame did not have a single endowed professorship in 1945. Today there are over 100. And the university now ranks in the top 22 of the nation's colleges and universities in terms of overall endowment, presently some $450 million.

The new buildings constructed while Hesburgh was president included O'Shaughnessy Hall of Liberal and Fine Arts and Nieuwland Science Hall, built during Hesburgh's first year as president.

I. A. O'Shaughnessy, president of Globe Oil and Refining in Minneapolis, contributed $2.1 million to build the first home for the university's largest academic division, the College of Arts and Letters. Over 20 years O'Shaughnessy gave Notre Dame more than $5 million as well as a large stock portfolio.

Twenty-four new buildings, four major renovations, and two additions to existing buildings changed the face of the campus between Hesburgh's first year as president and 1976. Besides O'Shaughnessy Hall and the Nieuwland Building, the new facilities included the Computing Center and Mathematics Building in 1962 and Memorial Library in 1963. That same year funds from the U.S. Atomic Energy Commission built the Radiation Research Building.

In 1968 the Athletic and Convocation Center —renamed the Joyce Athletic and Convocation Center in 1987 to honor Hesburgh's fellow Holy Cross priest, close friend, and longtime university executive vice president Edmund P. Joyce — opened for a variety of activities. The center included a basketball arena.

In the 1960s and early 1970s, Hesburgh and Notre Dame, along with the rest of the nation, were brought face to face with revolution and convulution. There were the Civil Rights movement; the Vietnam War and the opposition it spawned, particularly on college campuses; the changes in the Catholic Church following from the Second Vatican Council; and a general demand for greater individual self-expression. The latter resulted in a dramatic loosening of the paternal atmosphere and strict student rules at Notre Dame.

Hesburgh held firm on maintaining Notre Dame's right to prevent physical disturbances on campus, much to the dismay of some students and faculty, but in the fall of 1969 he signed an open letter asking the United States government to speed up its withdrawal of troops from Vietnam.

Two years earlier, he had taken a position that would remove direct control of Notre Dame from the religious community that had founded it 125 years earlier. He recommended to the Holy Cross community that the university's Board of Trustees, a self-perpetuating, six-man board whose members were all Holy Cross priests, be expanded and include laymen, and that the governance of Notre Dame be transferred to the Board of Trustees.

There were many reasons for the recommendation. There were now only 55 Holy Cross members among the over 500 teaching and research faculty at Notre Dame, laymen had taken on important administrative posts, and the university now had an annual operating budget of over $30 million, most of it derived from non-church sources, many of which were disturbed by the "clerical domination" of Notre Dame's administration. Hesburgh believed that the success of future fund raising depended on Notre Dame being lay-controlled and that such a change was in the spirit of the Second Vatican Council.

The Holy Cross community accepted his reasoning and a predominantly lay board of 30 trustees was established and control of the university was transferred to that board in 1967. However, it was provided that the president of Notre Dame would continue to

Joyce Athletic and Convocation Center, home of Fighting Irish basketball teams.

be a Holy Cross priest of the Indiana Province who would be subject to the board's appointment.

In 1988 there were 46 trustees, of whom only eight (including the Archbishop of Panama) were Holy Cross priests. Six trustees were women. Donald R. Keough, president of Coca-Cola; Henry G. Cisneros, mayor of San Antonio, Texas; and John Brademas, president of New York University, are among the trustees.

Two years before the change in ownership of the university, in 1965, two women became the first females to receive fulltime academic appointments at Notre Dame.

Six years later, the university announced in the fall of 1971 that it would accept women undergraduates in the 1972 freshman class. Ever since Notre Dame's founder Sorin had helped establish in the mid-1800s what became St. Mary's College, Notre Dame had a close relationship with the all-women's school, separated from Notre Dame's campus only by a highway. But it was 1972 when coeducation actually came to Notre Dame. The number of women in that entry group was limited to 365. Today, women make up about one-third of Notre Dame's undergraduate enrollment of some 7,600 students.

Also in 1971, the new Board of Trustees created a new position within the administration. The university provost ranked only behind the president and had direct control of academic affairs and indirect control of student affairs. The first occupant of the new office was James T. Burtchaell, a Holy Cross priest, theologian, and biblical scholar. He was succeeded in 1978 by a layman, Timothy O'Meara, who had been a mathematics professor at Notre Dame since 1962.

Hesburgh eventually eased a cap on undergraudate enrollment and there were over 8,700 undergraduate and graduate students at Notre Dame in 1976 with three-fourths of the undergraduates living on campus. Two high-rise residence halls, the first student residence buildings constructed in over a decade, had opened in 1969. Tuition in 1976 was $2,782, room and board $1,169.

When Hesburgh announced his retirement in 1986 at age 69, there were more than 9,700 students at Notre Dame — almost 7,600 undergraduate students and over 2,100 graduate and professional students. Undergraduate tuition for the 1988-1989 school year would be $10,325 with room and board averaging $3,075.

During his lengthy tenure as president, Hesburgh saw the school's annual operating budget increase from $9.7 million to $167 million along with the huge increase in the school's endowment. Hesburgh's successor said in June 1988 that Notre Dame receives "zero dollars from the Catholic church."

While the number of faculty had tripled in the Hesburgh years, their salaries had markedly increased with full professors averaging $56,000. Endowed scholarships had been $100,000 when Hesburgh took the reins. In his final year, they were $50 million. The university libraries had over 1.5 million volumes, compared to 250,000 in 1952.

Before leaving the president's post, Father Hesburgh had said Notre Dame in the future "will remain fiercely individual in style, unique in approach, and indelibly stamped by its Catholic heritage. In this way, Notre Dame will continue to serve as a bright light of learning and a reflective conscience of society."

In November 1986, Edward A. Malloy was named by the Board of Trustees to succeed Hesburgh the following spring. The candidates for the post included four other Holy Cross priests. Malloy was 46 when he was inaugurated as Notre Dame's 16th president on September 23, 1987.

Malloy, who had been associate provost for five years when he was named president, said 18 months into his term that his governing style was "collaborative".

At the time he was still living in two rooms on the first floor of the university's oldest student residence hall, Sorin, nearby the president's office in the Administration building. A hand-lettered sign saying "Welcome" goes on Malloy's door when he is home.

Malloy was known to students and faculty as "Monk", a childhood nickname, at the time he was named to head Notre Dame. He had come to Notre Dame from Washington, D.C., on a basketball scholarship. In high school at Archbishop Carroll he played on a team with John Thompson, coach of Georgetown University and 1988 United States Olympic basketball teams. Malloy, who still plays basketball on a regular basis, has said that in college he was "a slow player with a good jump shot."

Malloy holds a doctorate in Christian ethics from Vanderbilt University and was a tenured associate professor in the theology department when he was named associate provost.

At his inauguration as president, Malloy pledged to maintain the primary importance of academics at Notre Dame and promised to bring more women and members of ethnic and racial minorities to the university.

Notre Dame's successful fund raising continued under Malloy with a campaign for $300 million reaching 94 percent of the goal in one year.

A few months into his presidency, Malloy had introduced to a Notre Dame audience the president of the United States. In March 1988, President Ronald Reagan returned to the Notre Dame campus to speak at a ceremony noting the issuance at the Notre Dame post office of a stamp commemorating Knute Rockne. This was the first United States postage stamp in honor of a coach. Reagan had been on the campus earlier in his presidency when, in 1981, he and the now deceased actor Pat O'Brien, who played Rockne in the 1940 movie in which Reagan played George Gipp, received honorary degrees from Notre Dame.

Edward A. Malloy, C.S.C., president of Notre Dame University.

Notre Dame's O'Shaughnessy Hall of Liberal and Fine Arts.

A NOTRE DAME EDUCATION

The University of Notre Dame, which today emphasizes the "great university" theme, will celebrate its 150th anniversary in 1992. A university publication cites a major change in the school since World War II — "a striking transformation . . . from a modest and somewhat provincial undergraduate institution to a major university in four decades."

The emphasis on a great university is not without foundation.

The formulas for synthetic rubber were discovered at Notre Dame. The university pioneered in the study of germ-free animals in its Laboratories of Bacteriology at the Univeristy of Notre Dame (LOBUND), said to be at one time the world's leading biomedical germfree technology center. From here have come important contributions to research in cancer, heart disease, and gentic diseases, including hypertension and diabetes.

Notre Dame's chemical engineering department is highly ranked. The Radiation Laboratory on campus has the largest concentration of radiation chemists in the world.

Seventy percent of Notre Dame's preprofessional students are admitted to medical and dental schools, a figure double the national average.

Deans of the country's undergraduate business schools have ranked Notre Dame among the top 10 such schools. The department of accountancy shares a similar ranking. In a two-year period in the 1980s, only Harvard and Princeton produced more Rhodes Scholars than did Notre Dame.

Thirty-seven Notre Dame alumni are presidents of American colleges and universities. Notre Dame ranks in the top 10 of all schools represented among the nation's business leaders.

Still the university adheres to the vision of its founder, Father Edward F. Sorin, who in the 1840s sought to establish a great Catholic university in America. A university publication notes that "among the nation's major national universities, Notre Dame is the only one which stands firmly in the religious tradition in which it was founded." Today the University Archives or record center is a research facility for the study of American Catholicism.

Theodore M. Hesburgh, longtime Notre Dame president, has said that perhaps the one single thing that "nudged us into national academic prominence" was the decision following World War II to welcome to the campus "refugee scholars" from Europe who were fleeing "Stalin's Russia and Hitler's Germany." This resulted in the university, its former president said, "virtually overnight" taking on "the flavor of an international university."

"By providing refuge to European scholars who were seeking to retain their own freedom, Notre Dame liberated itself to enter the ranks of the world's major universities," Hesburgh said. "In doing so, it strengthened its own sense of intellectual purpose and anchored itself even more firmly in its religious tradition."

Actually, the wave of European scholars who came to Notre Dame began before the war. Over 40 came between 1930 and 1960. One group fled from Axis powers before World War II, another group came after the war, and a third group came in the 1950s.

Notre Dame's faculty, virtually all of whom hold doctor of philosophy degrees or its equivalent, includes many alumni who returned to teach after studying for graduate degrees, usually at other universities. In 1975 over a fourth of the 600 faculty were Notre Dame graduates. Where once priests comprised most of the faculty, in that same year 9 of 10 fulltime faculty members were laymen or women.

Today the undergraduate student to teaching faculty ratio is 12 to 1 and ninety percent of the undergraduate courses are taught by fulltime faculty members. The average class size is 29.

In recent years there has been an increase in "the intellectual caliber" of Notre Dame students. Thirty-five percent of the freshmen entering Notre Dame in 1987 ranked between one and five in their high school classes. Eight percent were in the top 10 percent of their classes; 94 percent were in the top 20 percent.

Notre Dame's undergraduates are enrolled in one of five academic divisions — the Freshman Year of Studies and four colleges. All of the university's some 1,800 freshmen are in the Freshman Year of Studies, which was inaugurated in 1961 and has its own dean. Freshmen take required courses in a curriculum which includes composition and literature, humanities, mathematics, foreign languages, natural science, history, and social science. They also take some elective courses.

Freshman academic advisors assist students who also may access a Freshman Learning Resource Center where small group review sessions, free tutoring, and class lectures on tape are available.

About 10 percent of a Notre Dame freshman class is supported by Reserve Officers Training Corps scholarships in the various branches of the armed services.

Ninety-eight percent of Notre Dame freshmen return for their sophomore year when they are enrolled in one of the four colleges. The largest is the College of Arts and Letters with over 2,300 undergraduate students studying in 16 academic departments which offer some 800 courses. Special and interdepartmental programs are also offered.

Degrees include bachelor of arts, bachelor of fine arts, bachelor of music, and a bachelor of arts/ bachelor of science in conjunction with the College of Science. Seventy percent of the students enrolled in the preprofessional program are admitted to medical and dental schools.

A professor of English says a goal of the College of Arts and Letters' faculty, which numbers 350, is to "teach students to subordinate their egos, at least for a moment, to something greater than the self."

Since 1980, the university has spent over 11 million dollars for construction and renovation of physical facilities for the fine arts and humanities. A $6.2 million faculty office building, Decio Faculty Hall, was built just north of Notre Dame Stadium and was dedicated in 1984.

Over 1,600 students are enrolled in the College of Business Administration, which has been ranked in the top 10 in the nation by a University of Virginia survey. This college has 100 faculty members teaching in four departments. Graduates receive the bachelor of business administration degree.

A Notre Dame business professor says, that no matter what the course, he talks "about taking a stand in life, about having morals and standards that will stand up to all kinds of tests (which students) will face in life."

The College of Engineering enrolls nearly 1,600 undergraduates who focus on such diverse areas as robotics, systems theory and microprocessors, computerized soil structure design and analysis, and catalytic and reaction engineering as well as the traditional engineering subjects. The faculty numbers 90. There are six departments and two special programs. Degrees received are the bachelor of science and the bachelor of architecture. The college's facilities include the new Fitzpatrick Hall of Engineering.

The smallest of the colleges is the College of Science, enrolling some 700 students. It first achieved national recognition some 60 years ago with the discovery of neoprene. This is the basic formula for the manufacture of synthetic rubber.

One of the college's objectives today, says its dean, a biochemist, is to "expose students to wanting passionately to make a significant contribution in life."

Twenty-one doctoral and 34 masters' degree programs are included in the graduate school within 29 university departments and institutes. There are some 700 graduate students in programs offered by the College of Arts and Letters.

Professional studies include two master of business administration programs in the College of Business Administration, a master of divinity degree in the department of theology, and a Law School offering the juris doctor degree.

The College of Business Administration has recently formed the Center for Research in Business, a $6.2 million endowment project aimed at positioning the college's graduate school among the top graduate programs in the country.

The Law School is the oldest law school under Catholic auspices in the United States. A $4-million, three-story expansion of the Law School building will add some 35,000 square feet of space. Offering the juris doctor degree, the Law School hosts several research institutes and centers including the Center for Civil and Human Rights, which holds all the papers written by Hesburgh during his 15 years association with the United States Civil Rights Commission.

Notre Dame has year-long foreign study programs, designed primarily for students in arts and letters and business, in Angers, France; Cairo, Egypt; Innsbruck, Austria; Mexico City, and Tokyo. There are similar programs, available from neighboring St. Mary's College in Rome and Maynooth, Ireland. Notre Dame has one-semester foreign study programs in Jerusalem and London, and a summer foreign language institute in Tianjin, People's Republic of China.

The University of Notre Dame today, says Kerry Temple, an alumnus and a writer for *Notre Dame Magazine,* is "classrooms full of young people studying things like particle physics, air flow dynamics, medieval literature, and blood coagulation . . . and more than 700 faculty members who know realms I've never entered. Like scouts," he said, "they guide these students to brave new worlds."

Decio Faculty Hall, the faculty office building on the Notre Dame campus.

NOTRE DAME ALUMNI

Even today, more than 50 years after his death, Knute Rockne, football player and coach, might still be Notre Dame's best known alumnus. And there are other famous football names. However, Theodore M. Hesburgh, the priest who headed Notre Dame for three-and-one-half decades, may have eclipsed Rockne's fame.

Many other Notre Dame's alumni have made their mark in many areas not related to athletics. Bruce Babbitt, former governor of Arizona, was a 1988 presidential aspirant. Secretary of Agriculture Richard Lyng is a Notre Dame graduate; so too Jose Napoleon Duarte, president of El Salvador; James Muller, a founder of International Physicians for the Prevention of Nuclear War, which won the 1985 Nobel Peace Prize; and the late Tom Dooley, the famous medical missionary.

Notre Dame alumni also have attained leadership roles in the church, business, and sports world. Others have been writers and entertainment figures. Among them are the late John Francis O'Hara and Archbishop Raymond Hunthausen of Seattle. O'Hara, former teacher, dean, and president at Notre Dame, became bishop of Buffalo after World War II and then was archbishop of Philadelphia, where he became the first member of the Holy Cross community to be named a cardinal.

There are also Edmund Haggar, chairman of the board, Haggar Apparel Co.; Donald Rice, head of Rand Corp.; John McHale, president of the Montreal Expos baseball team; Walter Kennedy, former chief executive of the National Basketball Association; the late Edwin O'Connor, author of *The Last Hurrah*; sports columnist Red Smith, also deceased; and Phil Donahue, television talk show host.

But Rockne remains the school's most publicized alumnus. He was identified with Notre Dame football to the extent that both he and the football program became national legends.

Rockne grew up on Chicago's northside in a Scandinavian neighborhood. He worked after high school to save money to attend college. At Notre Dame, he played varsity football and was a member of the track team. He also earned spending money as an "amateur" boxer.

After he graduated magna cum laude in chemistry, Rockne was asked to stay at Notre Dame as a chemistry instructor and assistant football coach. By 1918 he was head coach and athletic director. He is credited with making the school known to the country, even though Notre Dame's record in football before he took over was 145 and 40.

Rockne's Notre Dame teams, playing a national schedule, went 105-12-5 in the 13 seasons he coached before he was killed in a 1931 airplane crash in Kansas at age 43. Two of his teams were national champions, five were undefeated, and six lost only one game. The undefeated 1924 team beat Stanford in the Rose Bowl, Notre Dame's only appearance ever in that bowl game. That team featured a backfield which sportswriter Grantland Rice dubbed the "Four Horsemen."

A back on Rockne's first teams was George Gipp, who came to Notre Dame as a baseball player and became a national idol for his play on the football field. Gipp died in 1920 at age 25 of a strep-throat infection a few weeks after his final game at Notre Dame. Eight years later Rockne is said to have made a dramatic pregame speech to a Notre Dame team, asking them to "Win one for the Gipper."

The next best known Notre Dame football coach could actually claim to be one of the "Fighting Irish." Frank Leahy's successful 11-year coaching rein spanned the decade of the 1940s and included a 39-game win streak. Leahy had played football at Notre Dame under Rockne. He had been a lineman. As head coach, he was a driver and a detail man, Leahy was also known for his "exaggerated moralism." His manner of motivation worked, even with older students — many of Leahy's players were World War II veterans. Forty-two members of the 1947 Notre Dame team were to play professional football.

One writer has said the Leahy years "were an exciting, victorious, some would say fanatical, football era." During Leahy's time the school was accused of being a football factory, and school officials, including Hesburgh, often found themselves defending Leahy's success.

Actually, athletes at Notre Dame graduate at the same rate as the general student body — well over 90 percent in four years. Over the last 21 years, only six of 514 football players have not received degrees. In the past 17 years, every player on the men's basketball team has graduated.

Eventually, the job became too stressful for Leahy and he gave way to another Irishman, Terry Brennan, then 25, who enjoyed much less success.

Other alumni famous for their athletic feats include Hall-of-Fame-football players Alan Page (now a laywer living in Minneapolis), Paul Hornung, George Connor, and Wayne Millner, George Trafton, and Curly Lambeau (founder of the Green Bay Packers). The latter three are deceased.

One of the best known of recent Notre Dame pro football players is the now retired Joe Theismann, former Washington Redskins star and one of many well-known Notre Dame quarterbacks.

There were over 25 players from Notre Dame listed on 1987 National Football League preseason veterans rosters. They included New York Giants tight end Mark

Bavaro, Cincinnati Bengals defensive end Ross Browner, New York Jets linebacker Bob Crable, Cleveland Browns nose tackle Bob Golic, Minnesota Vikings guard Dave Huffman, San Francisco 49ers quarterback Joe Montana, and Atlanta Falcons guard John Scully.

Browner (1976 and 1977), Crable (1980 and 1981), Golic (1978), Huffman (1978), and Scully (1980) are among almost 70 Notre Dame football players who have been accorded All-America honors, dating back to Gus Dorais in 1913.

Notre Dame has also had nine basketball All-America players. The late Ed Krause, longtime Notre Dame athletic director, was a three-time All-America in the early 1930s. Present pro basketball star Adrian Dantley was chosen in both 1975 and 1976. Former pro players Austin Carr and John Shumate were All-America players in 1971 and 1974, respectively.

Former Notre Dame stars John Paxson and Kelly Tripucka are also currently playing pro basketball.

Notre Dame alumnus, Mark Bavaro, now a star tight end for the New York Giants.

The old and the new at Notre Dame — the Architecture Building at left, and the Snite Museum of Art.

ON CAMPUS

The University of Notre Dame occupies one of the nation's most attractive campuses. The Notre Dame campus is just north of South Bend, Indiana, near the Indiana-Michigan border. It is 90 miles east of Chicago.

Two lakes are on the north and northeast edge of the 1,250-acre campus. St. Joseph's Lake covers 26 acres and St. Mary's 17 acres. Since the transfer of legal governance of Notre Dame from the Holy Cross community to the university's Board of Trustees in 1967, the lakes are the approximate boundaries between the land to the south held by the university and that retained by the religious community.

Many of today's 96 college buildings occupy land once farmed by the Holy Cross community. As a history of the university says, "Notre Dame's principal endowment throughout much of its history has been its land."

One of the brothers who first came to Notre Dame with Sorin had been a farmer in France. On their arrival, about 10 acres had been cleared. Two years later, 120 acres was under cultivation to grow wheat, potatoes, and corn. Farm buildings went up along the shore of St. Mary's Lake. Not far away, livestock grazed.

The university's farms, staffed by Brothers of Holy Cross, at one time covered over 3,500 acres. Fifty-five buildings had been constructed for the farms. Some of the land was north of the campus, but in 1900 some 1,100 acres nearly bordered the campus. There were dairy herds, hogs, chickens, and fields of corn, alfalfa, wheat and potatoes. The university established an agricultural school in 1917 and awarded degrees in agriculture until 1932. Eventually the farms were all moved to a site in Granger, Indiana, eight miles to the north of the campus.

Anchoring the campus, itself, is the Administration Building or Main Building at the north end of the Main Quadrangle. The building which went up after the 1879 fire was the third building on the site. The famous dome was completed in 1883 and two wings were added later. Several renovations were made over the years.

Also a campus landmark is Sacred Heart Church on the Main Quadrangle just west of the Main Building. Constructed between 1871 and 1888, it was renovated in 1934 and again in 1968. In the center of the Main Quadrangle is the Edwin Sorin Memorial, a bronze statue of the university's founder.

Among the buildings on the east side of the Main Quadrangle are Washington Hall, the university's performing arts building, built in 1881 and recently renovated — a $1.6 million project; LaFortune Student Center, the Science Hall from 1883 until 1952 when the building was extensively renovated; Crowley Hall of Music, built in 1893 to house engineering classes, rebuilt after a 1916 fire and extensively renovated in 1976; and the Business Administration Building, constructed in 1932.

At the southeast corner of the Main Quadrangle is the Law School, originally built in 1930 with an addition added in 1972 and a three-story expansion just completed. Cushing Hall of Engineering and the new Fitzpatrick Hall of Engineering are immediately east of the Law School.

Buildings on the west side of the Main Quadrangle include the residence halls,

Sorin, built in 1888 and the first on campus to have private rooms; Walsh, built in 1909; and Alumni, which opened in 1931. Just north of Sorin is Corby Hall. Built in 1893, Corby was long a student residence hall but is now a residence for Holy Cross priests.

Other residence halls — Howard, Lyons, and Morrisey — were built in the 1920s on the South Quadrangle. Over the next three decades, seven residence halls were built to form a quadrangle northwest of the Main Quadrangle. There are dining halls on the South and North Quadrangles. The South Dining Hall is the building built in the late 1920s — it was finished in 1927 — and renovated in 1974. The North Dining Hall was built in 1957.

Notre Dame freshmen are required to live on campus, and 85 percent of all undergraduates live in campus residence halls.

There are presently 14 residence halls for men, the newest of which are two high-rise facilities, Flanner and Grace, built in 1969 at the northeast edge of the campus. Both house over 500 men. The oldest male residence hall is the original one, now called Sorin College.

The 11 residence halls for women include two opening in the fall of 1988. The new halls, Marion Burk Knott and Siegfried, are just south of the two high-rise halls. Other women's residences include Badin, called St. Joseph's when it opened in 1897 — it was renamed in 1917; the aforementioned Walsh, Howard, and Lyons; Lewis, opened in 1965; and Pasquerilla West and Pasquerilla East,

opened in 1981 and 1982, respectively, and located just south of the high-rise halls.

Each hall has a rector, most often a Holy Cross priest or brother in the men's halls, and at least one assistant rector along with a staff or resident assistants.

There are no social fraternities or sororities at Notre Dame and the residence halls are the focus of social, religious, and intramural athletic activities.

At the south end of the North Quadrangle is the Nieuwland Science Hall, constructed in 1952.

A more recent campus landmark is the Theodore M. Hesburgh Library, called Notre Dame Memorial Library when it was finished in 1963. On its south side, facing nearby Notre Dame Stadium, is a 132-foot-high stone mosaic mural of Christ as teacher with a huge representation of Christ with arms outstretched.

This mural has been seen many times on national television because Notre Dame's identity as a national institution, its alumni spread throughout the land, and its "subway alumni" make Notre Dame attractive to sponsors of televised sports events. Thus, hundreds of football games have been broadcast over the country from Notre Dame Stadium.

Some of those television viewers might know the Hesburgh Library mural as "touchdown Jesus," the gently irreverent description first given it by someone viewing it from inside the football stadium, someone who thought

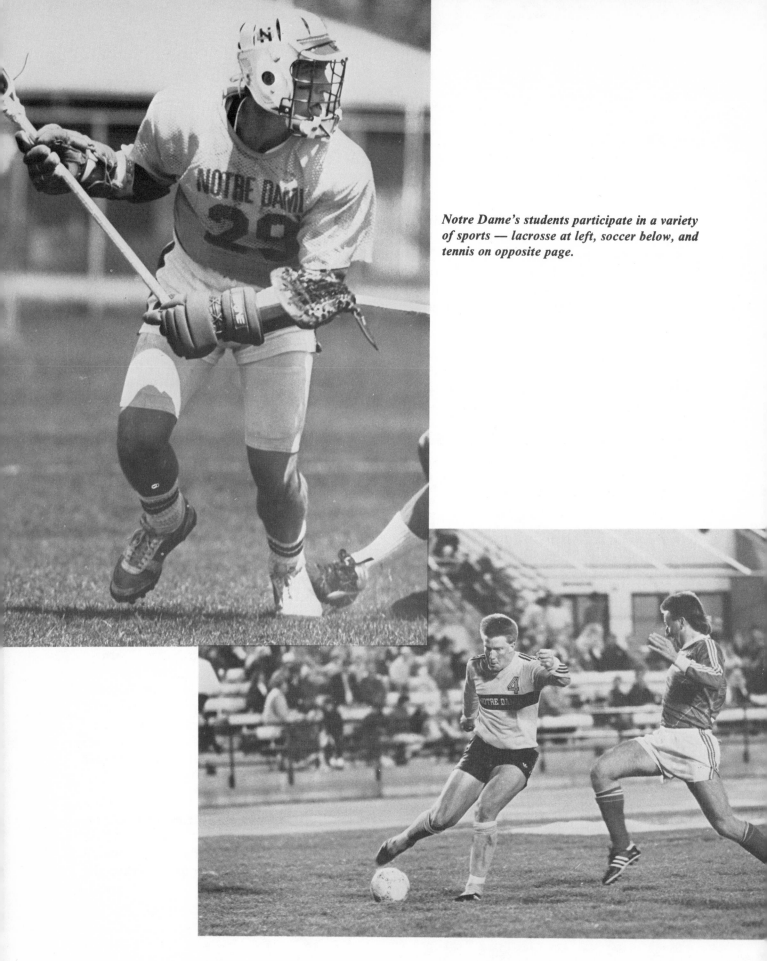

Notre Dame's students participate in a variety of sports — lacrosse at left, soccer below, and tennis on opposite page.

the pose similar to that of an official signaling a touchdown.

As for the library itself, it and six other libraries on campus hold more than 1.8 million volumes, one million microform units, 10,400 sound recordings, and they subscribe to 16,200 serials.

The university's Computing Center supports teaching and research as well as administrative and library applications. Terminals linked to the mainframe computer or minicomputers are located in several campus buildings. The computer facilities include a microcomputer laboratory.

Also on campus is the recently constructed $3.7 million Snite Museum of Art, with a collection of some 17,000 pieces ranging from ancient to contemporary art. The Notre Dame Press on campus is the largest Catholic university press in the world.

There are many institutes and centers on campus in addition to LOBUND and the Center for Business Research. Among the others are the Institute for Scholarship in the Liberal Arts, an $8.5 million project created by the university "to ensure high scholarship in the arts, humanities and social sciences."

One of 10 Notre Dame graduates volunteers to give one or more year of social service through programs coordinated by the university's Center for Social Concerns.

Away from the classroom, Notre Dame's students participate in a variety of campus organizations which include university fine arts and performing arts groups and over 150 special-interest clubs. Many activities are held in the newly renovated LaFortune Student Center. There are two student-run radio stations, a daily newspaper, and a weekly news magazine.

Recreational facilities include the 18-hole golf course at the southwest corner of the campus. There are outdoor tennis courts and a track; outdoor, lighted basketball courts; and playing fields on the west end of the campus for soccer, lacrosse, field hockey, rugby, and softball.

The huge Joyce Athletic and Convocation Center, the site of varsity basketball games, is adjacent to Notre Dame Stadium, home of the university's football team which, as does the men's basketball team, plays an independent schedule. The university fields men's varsity teams in 11 other sports. There are six women's varsity sports besides basketball. Most of the varsity teams at Notre Dame compete in the Midwestern Collegiate Conference.

The Joyce Center has basketball, tennis, and volleyball courts; an Olympic swimming pool; racquetball, squash, and handball courts; a track, an ice rink, a boxing room, and a weight room.

The 50-year-old Rockne Memorial Building at the west edge of the campus has basketball and volleyball courts, handball and racquetball courts, a swimming pool, and weight rooms.

There are six indoor courts in the Eck Tennis Pavilion.

The newest recreational facility, the Loftus Sports Center, opened in the fall of 1987.

ENTERING NOTRE DAME

"I invite you to join us here in this special place," Notre Dame President Malloy says in a university publication for prospective freshmen.

"As we look to the coming decade," Malloy wrote in 1987, "both society and the church will continue to face challenges in every area of human endeavor. What better place than Notre Dame to explore the full meaning of ethical notions like personal integrity and corporate responsibility.

"Together we will ponder nuclear deterrence and test tube babies, economic justice and global pollution. In library and laboratory, in the social interaction of the residence hall and the intense debate of the lecture hall, the spirit of Notre Dame will invigorate the common search for meaning and amelioration."

Malloy also told applicants to the university that "Notre Dame self-consciously and proudly proclaims itself to be a Catholic univer-

The ultimate goal — graduation.

LaFortune Student Center, site of many student activities at Notre Dame.

sity." Fewer than 10 percent of the university's students are non-Catholic. Notre Dame is the only one of the nation's major universities, another university publication points out, "which stands firmly in the religious tradition in which it was founded." Notre Dame, the university says, "is best characterized by its public commitment to the moral and spiritual values that undergird American society."

Applications to enter Notre Dame as an undergraduate are available in August for the following year's freshman class. The early application deadline is November 1 with those applicants notified in December. The regular application deadline is January 15 of the year the applicant will be a freshman. Notification is made from mid-March to early April. The confirmation date for admitted students is May 1.

Small group information sessions for prospective high school students and their parents are scheduled at regular times throughout the year and include campus tours. The tours also are available on weekdays during the summer. Notre Dame also has a hospitality program where during the college's regular academic year a high school senior stays overnight in a residence hall with a student host.

Transfer students must meet certain criteria

to apply and they are admitted at the fall semester only.

Criteria used in evaluating admissions to Notre Dame are quality of curriculum in the high school attended, class rank, concentration of talent in high school, scholastic aptitude (SAT) test scores, teacher's evaluation, extracurricular accomplishment, and an essay and personal statement.

The 1,820 freshmen entering Notre Dame in 1987 were among just under 3,100 who had been accepted from among the almost 8,000 who had applied. Some 9,600 students applied for the 1,800 places in the 1988 freshmen class.

One-quarter of the class entering Notre Dame in 1987 ranked in the top one percent of their high school class, 62 percent were in the top five percent, and 84 percent in the top 10 percent.

Thirty-five percent of the freshmen entering Notre Dame in the fall of 1987 were in the top five people in their high school graduating class. Eighty percent were in the top 10 percent. The average SAT scores of these freshmen were 580 verbal and 660 mathematics for a combined average of 1,230, almost 400 points more than the national average total score for high school seniors going to college.

Ten percent of the 1987 freshman class were minority students. Almost one-quarter were children of Notre Dame alumni. Thirty-six percent were women.

Thirty-nine percent of this class of 1991 were from states in the Midwest, 27 percent from Middle Atlantic states, 10 percent from the West, eight percent from the South, seven percent from New England, and six percent from the Southwest. The other three percent were international students.

The cost of attending Notre Dame as an undergraduate in the 1988-1989 academic year is estimated to be $14,800. Tuition and fees are $10,325 and room and board $3,075. The total for tuition and fees and room and board is $13,400. Graduate tuition is similar to the undergraduate figure. Law School tuition in 1987-1988 was $10,070.

The university says some two-thirds of the undergraduates at Notre Dame receive some form of financial aid. Total aid from all sources — scholarships, athletic grants-in-aid, loans, campus work study jobs, federal and state grants, and Reserve Officer Training Corps awards — totalled $34 million in 1987-1988. All financial aid administered by the university's Office of Financial Aid is awarded on the basis of need. The university has $20 million in endowment dedicated to minority scholarships.

Some 80 percent of the some 1,200 graduate and professional students at Notre Dame receive graduate and research assistantships, fellowships, scholarships, loans, and grants-in-aid. These totalled almost $18 million in 1987-1988.

For more information about the University of Notre Dame, you may call or write:

Office of Admissions
University of Notre Dame
Notre Dame, Indiana 46556

(219) 239-7505